Broken Dreams, Wounded Hearts

A Parent's Guide to Teenage Rebellion

Broken Dreams, Wounded Hearts

A Parent's Guide to Teenage Rebellion

by
Greg Glassford

Unless otherwise indicated, all Scripture quotations are taken from the *King James Version* of the Bible (KJV).

Scripture quotations marked *NAS* are taken from *The New American Standard Bible.* ©Copyright The Lockman Foundation, 1960, 1962, 1963, 1968, 1971, 1973, 1975, 1977.

Scripture quotations marked *AMP* are taken from *The Amplified Bible, New Testament.* ©Copyright 1954, 1958 by The Lockman foundations, La Habra, California.

BROKEN DREAMS, WOUNDED HEARTS

Greg Glassford
Youth Force International
P.O. Box 203
Broken Arrow, OK 74013

ISBN: 0-88368-244-3
Printed in the United States of America
©1987 by Greg Glassford

Whitaker House
580 Pittsburgh Street
Springdale, PA 15144

Dedication

With my heart filled with gratitude
and appreciation beyond my ability to
put into words,
I gratefully dedicate this book to my
loving parents,
Jim and Marge Glassford,
for their undeniable and compassionate
faith which enabled them to see the
future and not let go.

Thanks again, Mom and Dad.

Contents

Foreword

It was a cold October evening close to midnight when an eighteen-year-old boy pulled in to the gas station to phone his parents and inform them that he had arrived. When his mother and father heard the news, they shouted for joy after hanging up the phone simply because, in their estimation, what had just happened was truly a miracle — their son had come home.

Would you believe that just 30 days before all this occurred this young man had sworn to himself and his girl friend that he would never again step foot in Tulsa, Oklahoma, to be seen with his family of "Jesus Freaks"?

You see, from the time he entered the eighth grade until he turned eighteen years of age, this young man's life had evolved around alcohol, drugs, rock music, and his circle of friends. He was caught up in a world he thought nobody understood. Anyone who tried to interfere with him or his world did not do so without provoking a debate, conflict, or head-on collision.

In the eyes of his parents and many other adults, this young man was a prime example of the word *rebellious*. To abide by the rules established by those in authority over him was something he did only when he couldn't possibly avoid it. Even then, of course, he complied under protest. He simply abhorred submission to any form of outside control. For some reason, the words "resist the system" constantly flashed as a neon sign in his mind.

This was the kind of "son" over which his parents were now shouting for joy — one filled with anger, apathy, confusion, bitterness, and resentment. This son used to steal money from his father's struggling business. This son had ruined two of three family cars while out partying. From time to time, this son had pushed his mother around, beat up his brother, and filled his sisters with fear. Through his devious lies and clever manipulations, this son had been able to lead his parents to believe almost anything.

Although various rules had been laid out for him to obey, this particular son had ignored them most of the time. He had continually "bucked" authority. For a long time, his parents had not had a "handle" on him. For years, he had made their home life intolerable. Yet this was the son over whom they shouted for joy when he called to announce his arrival from Florida.

What caused these parents to maintain such an attitude of faith, hope, and love towards their son who had so dishonored them and who had brought such constant confusion, disappointment, and division into their lives? How could they welcome such a rebel into their abode with open arms after all the heartbreak and devastation he had caused them?

Awaiting the arrival of his mother to escort him home to face his father with whom he had maintained an ongoing feud for years, the young man saw the family station wagon turn the corner. As it drew closer he noticed that the person driving was not his mother, as he had expected. Instead, the solitary figure of his father was clearly evident behind the wheel.

Not knowing exactly what his dad would say or do, the young man grew a bit uneasy as the car pulled up next to his. The father got out of the vehicle and the son began walking toward him somewhat hesitantly. Approaching within arm's length, the young man reached out his hand to offer a manly handshake, when suddenly to his surprise his father pushed his hand away — only to grab him up in a bear-hug of love, acceptance, and forgiveness.

Fighting back the tears, the young man sensed that something was different about his dad. There was something new and genuine about him. He could feel a love and power his father had never before possessed or expressed.

I can never forget that night. And I'm sure that Dad can never forget it either.

It was the night that my father, Jim Glassford, and I started the long road to friendship, unity, and (most of all) a relationship of true love based on Jesus Christ, the healer of broken hearts.

Before the final miracle of my salvation came to pass, things seemed to grow worse instead of better. But because my parents saw the future and wouldn't let go, eight months later my life was transformed.

On a very special Sunday night, I asked the Lord to change my life, and He did. That very evening I was saved, filled with the power of the Holy Spirit, delivered from the bondages of nicotine, drugs, and alcohol — and called into the ministry to preach the Gospel!

Having experienced teenage rebellion firsthand in my own life, and having been in full-time ministry for ten years, I have felt an urgency to share on paper what is in my heart concerning this vital and timely topic. That is the reason for this book.

I pray that as you read these pages the precious Holy Spirit will lead you into all truth and wisdom regarding your present situation and that He will begin to reveal to you where to start in seeing total restoration of your strained or broken relationship(s).

I also pray that as you read this book you will receive hope and vision to see the impossible become possible and the hopeless become truly hopeful.

God bless you.

— Greg Glassford

Introduction

After Lucifer (Satan) rebelled against God and was cast out of heaven to the earth (Is. 14:12), apparently many years passed before God made man in His own image. Then Adam and Eve were created and given dominion over all the works of God's hands. (Gen. 1:26-28.)

After some time, the day came when Satan came into the garden to deceive man. Most people know the story from there on. Satan convinced Eve that she should eat the forbidden fruit, then Eve convinced Adam to join her in her act.

From that point on, the results are history. The first couple ate of the fruit in direct disobedience to God, and mankind has been adding to that sin ever since.

As an introduction to this book, let me give an illustration of the point I would like to make about the state of our present-day society.

What would happen if you dropped a brand new car into the ocean? Well, it obviously would get very wet. If the car were removed immediately, perhaps it could be salvaged, possibly repaired, and used for many miles to come.

But suppose the car were left in the ocean for a month. What would it look like then? What about after one year? Two years? Seven years? Twenty years? One hundred years? Are you beginning to get the picture?

The longer that new car stayed on the bottom of the ocean, the more exposure it would have to salt water, and the more it would corrode. The powerful underwater currents most likely would beat the car up as well, not to mention the effects of thousands of living organisms in the ocean looking for a new home to which to become attached.

I am saying that, through the years, mankind has gotten more and more corrupt and rebellious. It took a few years after the fall of Adam and Eve for man to begin to make idols. But many people still believed in Jehovah God. Things have gotten so far out of hand today, however, that millions do not even believe in the existence of the supernatural realm, much less in God or His Son, Jesus, the Savior of the world.

To some extent then, the state of rebellion in which this young generation of the 1980s exists can be blamed on preceding generations — to be more precise, the generation directly preceding this one. Let's face it, parent, the behavior of children is a direct result of the way they have been trained.

Proverbs tells parents that they should **train up a child in the way he should go...,** promising them that if they will do so, **...when he is old, he will not depart from it** (Prov. 22:6). Well, if there is a *way a child should go*, there is also a way he *shouldn't* go.

What does that phrase, *to train up a child*, mean? Although this book is not primarily concerned with rearing children, we cannot talk about teenage rebellion and disregard the home scene.

I am thoroughly convinced that most teenage rebellion could be halted *if parents would dare to be doers of the Word and not hearers only.*

A quarter of the children in America now will be raised in single-parent homes, most of them without a father. Many marriages which have not ended in divorce are living "hell holes." Many children are being raised in homes where all they know is that parents fight all the time.

Togetherness, communication, family outings, meals together, family prayer, love, and forgiveness are unheard of in so many homes today. Because mothers and fathers have never set standards for living in their own lives, children are raised with no idea that godly characteristics are possible, much less desirable.

Other parents give their children good moral instruction — but live in a contradictory way.

"Do what I say," they tell their off-spring, "not what I do."

Of course, it is good to instruct children in the right way of living, but if parents are not living that way in front of their children, most of the time verbal instruction is wasted.

Good or bad, the most effective message is the lifestyle which a child sees. What children *see* in their parents is what will determine the success or failure of their training.

As one preacher put it, "The greatest sermon is the one that walks and talks and breathes."

I have ministered personally to hundreds of young people raised in church, with many of them "PKs." (preacher's kids), whose hearts were harder than any I have seen in children raised in worldly cultures!

These teens are *victims of circumstances*.

Children were created to conform, and they will do just that. They will conform to the strongest influences impressed upon their hearts and minds. Paul tells us in Romans 12:2, **Be not conformed to this world....** Well, if we are not to conform to *this* world, what world are we to conform to? Romans 8:29 tells us that God predestined us to become **...conformed to the image of his Son....** But is that conformation to the image of God's Son taking place in the homes of most Christians today? Do our teens today have good Christian role models to mold their lives after?

Because of continual compromise on the part of earlier generations, including ours, standards today have slipped, compromise has crept into the Church and home, and teenagers are being swept away in a mass of confusion and rebellion. A child's outlook on life, his world view, will determine the quality of his decisions and will determine what he does, says, and wears, who his friends are, and where he goes.

Everyone is impressionable, but adults are not as impressionable, of course, as children and teens. When a young person is searching for an identity in life and cannot seem to find it through the ones closest to him — his parents — many wrong responses can be the outcome. For many teenagers, the reaction has been bitterness, which leads to resentment, which leads to hatred, which results in rebellion.

As adults, we owe the teenagers of this generation an apology for the way we have failed them. We also owe them better examples to follow.

Will you and I agree and determine to be the examples our teenagers so desperately need today?

That is the question I hope to raise — and answer — in the pages of this book.

1
Close to Home

Todd was always a well-behaved young man. He loved and respected his mother and father more than any other people in the world. He always showed the highest sense of appreciation for his parents. He was proud of his father and honored his mother. The family life of Todd and his parents was one of real fulfillment — until something happened.

Almost overnight it seemed that Todd became cold and hard. Rebellious, you might say. Disrespect for his parents, teachers, and other authority figures began to become a way of life for this once "nice young man." An obvious attitude of "I could not care less about your opinion" set in, as apathy began its deadly work.

Today Todd is full of rebellion. He has little desire to cooperate with anyone who tries to tell him what to do. He has become what the adult world calls a "rebel." But why? Why is he rebellious? What happened to trigger this sudden change of attitude and behavior?

Sarah's family is at the end of their rope in trying to deal with this undisciplined, disoriented, and, to say the least, highly disturbed young lady. Her foster parents say, "We have tried everything, and nothing seems to satisfy her."

Abandoned at birth and unable to cope with her lack of identification, Sarah has gone from foster home to foster home, causing continual chaos every place she sets her feet. All her brief life, she has been slashing back at society because of something very frustrating and dissatisfying within her innermost being — her heart, the place where the joys and pains of life are stored. Like Todd, Sarah is also labeled "rebellious."

Thousands of young people all over the world who have similar — or extremely different — situations carry the same label: rebel. Outwardly, rebellion is clearly seen and noted. We do not have to look very far to witness the expression of one who defies that which he finds unacceptable.

But what is going on behind the *seen*? What has so disturbed millions of teens to the point of rebellious living such as has never been experienced in any other generation?

The answer lies within the heart. Jesus said, **"...For the mouth speaks out of that which fills the heart"** (Matt. 12:34b NAS). At times I like to paraphrase that verse like this: "For out of the overflow of the heart, *the life lives.*"

Rebellion is the reaction from the heart of one who has not been able to cope with such things as a broken home, a tragedy involving a close friend or relative, the lack of parental trust, constant confusion concerning self-identification and self-worth, the breaking up of a close friendship, and so forth. The list of problem situations which many teens face and which may cause rebellious reactions could go on and on.

When a teenager experiences one or more of these situations in life, it brings upon him varying degrees of hurt, pain, and rejection. When these emotions are not dealt with in the proper fashion, most likely the result will be an emotional and usually socially unacceptable outburst or reaction. In many cases, unless something is done to rectify the situation, an entire lifestyle of rebellion can develop.

What about the parents? To say the least, there is a tremendous amount of frustration and hurt, and a feeling of total disarray on the part of parents when their child begins this rebellious way of life. Most parents are caught off guard and are unprepared to properly handle such situations. The result is usually some sort of "separate and equal reaction" instead of a "wise response." Thus, kindling is added to the fire of rebellion until it roars out of control.

What is a parent to do in the face of all this? Where should, where can, he or she turn? Certainly the parent loves the child, but what is the first step toward reconciliation and restoration? What is the first step in bringing healing to the broken parent-child relationship?

Obviously, we must look far beyond the surface into the realm of the *unseen* if we are ever going to be able to effectively minister life, love, and freedom to the millions of young people and their parents who are victims of teenage rebellion: a problem of the heart.

2
Who's to Blame?

Realizing that there are various levels, causes, and degrees of rebellion, for the most part the question of "who's to blame anyway?" will usually remain unanswered.

When rebellion against parents flares up in the life of a teenager causing their relationship to begin to crumble, who *is* to blame? It must be somebody's fault, we reason. Who started this thing anyway?

We are always wanting to know exactly who did what, when, and why. In some cases, knowing the answers to these questions can help to resolve serious conflicts and problems, especially if it concerns certain isolated incidents.

But when dealing with a lifestyle of rebellious attitudes which have caused broken hearts, bruised emotions, and serious complications which will affect the future of all parties involved, the most important question is not so much "who's to blame?" as it is *"what's* to blame?"

If you are faced with a situation in which a child you love has developed a regular and noticeable rebellious attitude, whether slight or serious, you should be honest with yourself and admit that the fault lies with both child and parent. No matter who is most at fault, love never keeps score. Both parties have "missed it" somewhere, somehow.

Does it really matter who's most responsible?

Let me exhort you to begin concentrating your efforts on healing the open wounds between you and your child, **...forgetting what lies behind and reaching forward to what lies ahead** (Phil. 3:13 NAS).

Sometimes we are too quick to judge ourselves, even to the point of irreversible behavior. When we are cornered by the hurt and heartbreak of a rebellious child, we might say, "He'll never change." Or

26

then again, we might think, "I can never forgive her for all she has done to me."

But if the Lord Jesus Christ truly lives in our hearts, nothing should ever get that bad.

If, per chance, you have said or thought such things as these, pause right now and go before the Lord to ask His forgiveness. As you do so, you will begin to feel the additional strength, healing, and courage you will need to see this thing through to victory.

Hope will begin to rise up within you again as you realize that you are *not alone*.

3
What Causes
Teenage Rebellion?

There are many, many things which may cause rebellious actions in the life of a teenager. Though we will not be able to go into great detail concerning all of these areas, I would like for us to explore some of the predominant causes of teenage rebellion which I have observed in the years of my ministry.

Peer Pressure

How often have parents been frustrated when their teen gives as the reason (or excuse) for his actions the "fact" that "everybody's doing it." Among teens, it sometimes seems that everything — fashion, dating, music, entertainment, food and drink, even hairstyle — is dictated by "the group."

How should parents realistically respond to this kind of conformist reasoning from their child who is seemingly looking only for acceptance by his peers?

I think it is vitally important to ask why this particular argument is even used by teens. Why is what "everybody" is doing so very, very important to teenagers?

In order to answer these questions, we must first come to understand that adolescence is the age of identity when young people begin the adventure of truly discovering who they are and where they "fit in." In the mind of a teenager, the thought of isolation, of standing alone in opposition to the group, is not only unappealing but even quite threatening. To the vast majority of young people, group approval means everything. Very few are born leaders. Fewer still have any real desire to go against the crowd on important issues.

This natural tendency to conform is not limited to teens. Throughout the years, *society* has been guilty of fashioning our taste in many things, such as cars, clothing, and even politics, education and religion. How many times do we, as adults, act on our own personal principles regardless of what other people think or say or do? The truth is that in many cases we adults are just as guilty of group conformity as our children are. The old cliche' about "keeping up with the Jones" applies more to adults than it does to adolescents.

Radical reactions to a child's tendencies to give in to peer pressure may result in further separation and withdrawal. The popular parental response, "Do what I say just because I say so!" will always remain counter-productive. It may result in winning the battle but losing the war.

If you have been guilty of using this type response to your child's questioning of your decisions, let me suggest that you begin deepening your answers through application of the following communication and teaching methods. Turn a potentially rebellious situation into a learning opportunity by challenging your youngster to think for himself. When he claims that "everybody's doing it," instead of reacting with sarcasm or criticism, try one of these responses instead:

"Is everybody *really* 'doing it'? Who isn't? Why not?"

"Why is this point of view so important to you?"

"Is 'everybody' ever wrong?" (By looking at the life of Jesus, we can see that truth is often in the minority.)

"What is more important to you, doing what is right, or doing what *the group* is doing?"

"Is it wrong to be different?"

"Are there groups of 'everybodies' which should be avoided?"

"Whose opinion is most important to you — that of your boy/girl friend, peers, mom, dad, teachers, neighbors, other Christians, pastor, God?"

"What will it take for you to stand up for what you believe is right?"

"Are you able to 'swim against the tide' with confidence?"

Security is a key word in the life of a young person. Most teens find security through acceptance by *the group*. As long as they look, talk, and move just like everybody else, they feel there will be less friction and opposition — thus, more security.

As you begin to discuss these questions with your child in an attitude of gentleness, honesty, and understanding, not only will you help him begin to develop his own values, but, more importantly, you will help him to develop a genuine sense of security in the surrounding of his own home.

Lastly, you will begin to notice rising up in your child a fresh courage to do what is right even when he is surrounded by a world doing what is wrong.

Parental Provocation

And, fathers, do not provoke your children to anger; but bring them up in the discipline and instruction of the Lord.

Ephesians 6:4 NAS

To provoke means to anger, irritate, or annoy. The word implies the stirring up and arousing of feelings and actions.

I think that from time to time we are all manipulators, both teens and parents included. Sometimes we both make attempts to manipulate each other in order to "get our own way."

Sometimes this manipulation may be so subtle that the parent or child is not even aware he is using it. But when we as parents become conscious that we are being manipulative, it is time for us to confront our manipulation and deal with it.

A good example of provoking a child to anger can be found in this area. Parents sometimes utilize manipulation when they "threaten" to withhold certain privileges from their child if he doesn't measure up to their set standard of behavior. This kind of parent has a certain way of almost blackmailing the child to "get with the program" by constantly reminding him, "Do it or *else!*"

God's reward system is always filled with hope, not threats. There are times when discipline is in order, of course, and we will discuss this topic in a later chapter. But what I am referring to here is an action of revenge which will stir up and provoke a child to anger. Any time a command is given without proper reasoning or compassionate explanation, or in an attitude of anger and disgust, it will create wrath in the child and will contribute to a declining relationship.

The dictionary defines *manipulation* as controlling or playing on by artful, unfair or insidious means, especially to one's own advantage.

Bringing up old errors, mistakes, and failures from the past to use as "testimony" against your child will cause him to become angry. This recourse to past "sins" seems justifiable when the child begins to question your credibility, but no one likes to be reminded of his past shortcomings. You must always remember that you are the parent; only you have the maturity and experience to see beyond this temporary crisis to the desired resolution.

The only positive solution is to be clear and consistent in your expectations, rules and discipline. Allow the fruit of the Spirit to dominate and determine your actions and reactions by placing in the hands of the Lord any bad attitude you may have toward the child, along with any desire to "get even" with him.

Lack of Parental Trust

Sometimes parents fail to allow their teenage children the freedom to begin to make certain decisions on their own and to voice their opinions on matters that concern them — which is the usual response in the case of rebellion.

When a child enters adolescence, he begins to realize, "Hey, I've got a will too!" The responsibility of the godly parent is to help mold and shape that young will after the character of Jesus. One thing this great responsibility demands is a certain amount of freedom for the teen, and a truckload of faith and trust from the parent(s).

In working with troubled kids over the years, I have found that many of them rebelled because the demands of their parents were too stringent and too rigid. Some parents become "unbending," and do not allow for the growth and change their young person goes through as he matures and develops. We cannot expect the same kind of "instant obedience" from a thirteen-year-old that might be appropriate for a child of three or four years of age.

If a parent refuses to allow his child to grow up and exercise some independence, a negative cycle will begin to manifest itself. As the parent becomes more unreasonable and unyielding, the child will begin to develop a "guilt-ridden" complex. The more hopeless he feels, the worse he acts, because he doesn't really know how to express the frustration he feels inside. And the worse the child acts, naturally the more determined the parent becomes to force him to behave.

But what do you as a parent do when all trust seems lost because of your child's constant abuse of certain liberties granted him? The answer is: Never stop trusting! You may not be able to trust him in some major areas at this time, but always provide something whereby your child can "prove himself" again and again. It may be something seemingly as insignificant as taking a letter to the mailbox — but always keep the door of trust open. (We will be looking at more helps in this area in a later chapter entitled "Building a Strong Relationship with Your Teenager.")

Lack of Proper Upbringing

I believe one of the most devastating philosophies to ever hit our nation is the humanistic ideology which holds that spanking a child will frustrate him and warp his mind. Parallel with this philosophy is the theory that spanking a child teaches him to hit others and eventually causes him to become a violent person.

You must make a decision as to what you are going to believe and act upon.

Because so many millions of parents have trusted in and relied upon these, and other, worldly concepts in rearing their offspring, the result has been a generation of undisciplined, irresponsible and rebellious children.

Let us hear what the Word of God has to say on this subject of child-rearing:

Train up a child in the way he *should go***: and when he is old, he will not depart from it** (Prov. 22:6).

Foolishness (rebellion) is bound in the heart of a child; but the rod of correction shall drive it far from him (Prov. 22:15).

Chasten thy son while there is hope, and let not thy soul spare for his crying (Prov. 19:18).

Withhold not correction from the child: for if thou beatest him with the rod, he shall not die. Thou shalt beat him with the rod, and shalt deliver his soul from hell (Prov. 23:13,14).

He that spareth his rod hateth his son: but that loveth him chasteneth him betimes (Prov. 13:24).

Spanking is only one of many effective means of disciplining a child. In itself, without the proper love and understanding, spanking can produce unfortunate and negative results — as has happened many times in the past. But utilized in the proper manner, spanking is part of God's plan to raise up children full of self-discipline, self-respect, integrity, character, and responsibility.

The lack of proper upbringing has been the result of deteriorating generations. Why have so many parents failed to bring up their children in the nurture and admonition of the Lord?

As you study nature, you will find that God has equipped most animals with an in-born fear of things which might be harmful to them. Their survival depends on recognition of a particular danger in time to avoid it.

But the frog seems to have been absent when the "distant early warning systems" were being passed out. If a frog is placed in a pan of lukewarm water under which the heat is very gradually being increased, he will typically show no great desire to escape. Since he is a cold-blooded creature, his body temperature remains the same as the water around him so he doesn't notice the slow change taking place. As the temperature continues to intensify, the frog will remain totally unaware of the danger. He could easily hop to safety, but usually he seems oblivious to what is going on. He will just sit there "adjusting to the situation" — until it is too late. Eventually, the boiling frog will "pass on to his reward," having fallen prey to an unnecessary misfortune he could easily have avoided.

Sometimes we can be like the frog. We are quick to respond and react to sudden dangers that confront us such as wars, epidemics, fires, floods, earthquakes, tornadoes, and hurricanes which bring instant devastation. However, if a threatening situation arises slowly, very slowly, perhaps over a number of years, we often allow ourselves to "boil in ignorance."

Without the slightest croak of protest, we have passively accepted a slowly deteriorating young generation. Suppose the parents of yesterday could make a brief visit to our world to observe the conditions that prevail among our children. I believe they would certainly be appalled and dismayed by the widespread juvenile problems which have been permitted to develop.

Something, or someone, has "messed up" somewhere. I believe the key to rectifying this situation lies in the proper upbringing of our children.

Instead of submitting their families to the Lord Jesus Christ and following His Word, many Christians have been swayed to another system of rule which is strictly in opposition to the righteous way and strongly supportive of the worldly way. The result has been tragic, yet we have been warned for centuries:

If ye be willing and obedient, ye shall eat the good of the land:

But if ye refuse and rebel, ye shall be devoured with the sword: for the mouth of the Lord hath spoken it.

Isaiah 1:19,20

I do not believe the answer to the rebellion in your child lies in giving him a whipping. For some younger teens, it may still have a beneficial effect, but for most teens it will be looked upon as a joke and will create a negative counter reaction which will only add to your problem instead of solving it. I do, however, believe in establishing a strong balance for rules and discipline for the teenage rebel. (We will look at this balance in depth in a later chapter.)

Another cause of teenage rebellion can be seen through the highly visible and easily available...

Media

You've probably read someplace that young people will spend many, many hours in front of the television set in the course of their elementary, junior high school, and high school years. A recent study revealed that the average American child will have watched 17,000 hours of television by the time he has reached the age of 18.[1] When you calculate that into days, it averages out to 708 straight days, or 23.5 solid months — which is close to a full two years of non-stop t.v. watching!

Although there are some very positive, upbuilding and edifying programs on the air, it must be admitted that the television medium has been one of the most subtle means of slowly but obviously introducing the American public to a lifestyle of sin and degradation.

Years ago, when commercial television was still in its infancy, those in charge of its programming held such high moral standards that a man and a woman, even when their t.v. roles portrayed them as husband and wife, could not be filmed together in the same bed! (Remember Rob and Laura Petrie of the old "Dick Van Dyke Show"? How about Lucille Ball and Desi Arnaz in "I Love Lucy"? My, my, how things have changed!)

---

[1]*GROUP Magazine*, Feb. 1987, p. 12.

You know the way it is today. Sensuality, lust, and perversion have flooded prime time television. Adultery, premarital sex, homosexuality, and male and female unwed roommates are not only accepted "norms" of behavior, but, in many cases are promoted and encouraged as "alternative lifestyles."

ROCK MUSIC with its highly violent, openly suggestive, and blatantly rebellious overtones has stormed the world of the young, "preaching" to our teenagers (and now younger children) to "be your own god" and "fight for the right to party."

Parents everywhere are now beginning to rise up in protest against many bands and against some of the albums which are being sold in local record shops nationwide. With song titles and lyrics becoming more and more explicitly sexual, violent, and drug-centered, it is no wonder that more and more parents, teachers, ministers, and other responsible adults are becoming increasingly concerned about what is being poured into the ears and minds of our young people.

I could fill literally pages and pages of this book with degrading rock titles and lyrics, as well as with transcripts of interviews and attested philosophies of numerous, highly popular, and virtually worshipped rock idols. The point is that young people everywhere are feeding upon an ungodly type of music which openly promotes everything from illicit sex to Satan worship.[2]

Secular rock music has definitely played a significant role in both the creation and stirring up of a rebellious attitude in the hearts of American teenagers. The Lord Jesus taught His disciples, **Take heed what ye hear...** (Mark 4:24). This means that we are to be careful and alert as to what we allow to enter the gate of our eardrums.

We become like that with which we associate: **...evil communications corrupt**

---

[2]For detailed information on this topic, please write our ministry.

good manners (1 Cor. 15:33). We are what we eat. The longer a young person "feeds on" rebellious resources such as rock music, the more his moral character will be eaten away. He will eventually become like the thing which he constantly takes into his mind and spirit: **For as he thinketh in his heart, so is he...** (Prov. 23:7).

Just a quick word of warning to you if you have a child who is an avid listener to rock music. Understand that this medium is one of Satan's highest forms of deception, influence, and manipulation. To continue to allow your child to listen to all the rock music he wants to hear without limit is a very dangerous practice and a bad mistake.

However, pray about how you should handle the situation. Don't act like a bull in a china closet, or you just might increase the rebellion problem in a moment's time.

I encourage you to begin by placing the facts before your child, monitoring his listening activity, and screening his album purchases by content as well as by price.

Absentee Parents

In the book, *Parents & Teenagers,*[3] there is an article by Jay Kesler entitled "Absentee Parents." I feel inspired to share part of this article with you here:

"The demands of our culture have created a situation in which more and more young people are being raised by absent parents. In fact, in any group of ten teenagers, you'll find that six or seven of them live in a home where there is some disjuncture. In its most serious form it involves divorce or the death of one or both parents. In other situations it involves alcoholism, emotional illness, or time abuse.

"The term *workaholism* has been coined to describe one form of time abuse. The well-known football commentator John Madden said on national television that he left coaching because one day his wife said she was taking their son to get his driver's license, and he

---

[3](Wheaton, Illinois: Victor Books, a division of SP Publications, 1984), pp. 475, 476.

thought the boy was still twelve years old. He had been so caught up in his work that he had missed four years of his son's life. This happens with a lot of parents, and I give Madden a great deal of credit for leaving a prominent career to devote more time to the more important concerns of his family.

"Today about half of the mothers in America are working, and many of the fathers are traveling. Inevitably, a large number of children are being raised by absent parents...."

Although there are some "super-kids" who are able to cope with this kind of situation with an understanding that Mom and Dad have to work to put food on the table, clothes on their backs, and a roof over their heads, there are still multitudes of young people who are not so strong and, if they could change the situation around, would do so to have Mom and Dad home more often.

I have ministered to a good number of teenagers who have grown bitter and rebellious toward their parents simply because the parents are not around when the youngsters need them the most. When does a teen need his parents the most? Right now!

In other words, when an important situation comes up, and the child needs counseling, guidance, and wisdom, how long will he have to wait to get it from his parents? Schedules of both teen and parent often conflict to the extreme that days can go by when neither one sees much of the other.

Have you possibly built an invisible wall between yourself and your child because of your busy schedule? When was the last time your teen approached you with an important question concerning his future or a pressing issue, or to ask for your opinion of something, in a sincere effort to seek your approval? If these times have been rare, then I think it's high time that you begin to re-evaluate your schedule and manage your time in a bit wiser manner before you too wake up to find out that your "twelve-year-old" son (or daughter) is going down to get a driver's license!

The Broken Home

Unfortunate as it may be, divorce and separation are perhaps two of the major causes of rebellion and broken-heartedness in the life of youth today.

Recently, I was ministering in Minnesota at a youth retreat with a number of teens and leaders. The first night as I glanced across the crowd, I saw a typical sight. A young lady about sixteen years of age was sitting near the back of the room with an expression of hurt, bitterness, and obvious rebellion written all over her face.

Although the Holy Spirit was moving in a mighty way during the services, with many young people breaking down before the Lord and receiving their miracle of release and restoration, nothing seemed to sway this girl's countenance in the least.

As a matter of fact, things looked worse as the weekend continued. Near the close of the very last meeting, I felt a strong urge in my spirit to talk to this young lady at the conclusion of the service.

Throughout the weekend, many counselors had tried to talk to her, pray with her, and to find out what was troubling her. I already knew what a challenge I was facing, so I prayed that the Lord would minister to her through me.

Sure enough, as I approached her, the first words to come out of my mouth were, "You've got to give your mom another chance."

Even as I was speaking, the young lady began to weep convulsively. Then she sobbed, "I can't."

I counseled with her for a few moments, then I prayed for a miracle.

You see, this young lady's rebellion was a direct result of a broken heart. When divorce hits a home, hurt begins to fly everywhere. Much of the time, the parents are hurting so much, both for themselves and their children, they begin to feel resourceless, empty, and without the right words to say. Therefore, many teens never really receive proper spiritual care during this trying time. The help that is offered through friends and relatives often represents nothing more than a frustrated swirl of emotionalism.

In such cases, all of a sudden the child is with only one parent when just a few hours or days before, he had two. Because of confusion and mixed, scattered emotions, one of the only resorts for a teen is withdrawal. He begins to hide his emotions and starts regressing into his own world, one which only he understands — some of the time.

No condemnation is intended for those who have experienced the trauma of divorce, either as parents or children. Very possibly you have seen these same things in your own family. I simply desire to communicate what some teens go through at a time like this.

Although these and other causes create a portion of the rebellion which we see in youth today, there are realistic measures to take to begin the restoration process and to reunite our children with the Lord and with ourselves.

4
Natural Weapons Won't Win Spiritual Battles

Finally, my brethren, be strong in the Lord, and in the power of his might.

Put on the whole armour of God, that ye may be able to stand against the wiles of the devil.

For we wrestle *not against flesh and blood,* but against principalities, against powers, against the rulers of the darkness of this world, against spiritual wickedness in high places.

Ephesians 6:10-12

(For the weapons of our warfare are not carnal, *but mighty through God to the pulling down of strong holds;*).

2 Corinthians 10:4

Although we acknowledge that there are things of the past that we would change if we could...although we face and admit that we've made mistakes concerning our children...although we begin to adjust our schedule to spend

55

more time with our kids...although our teens begin to follow the rules to contribute to a joint effort to make things right, and...although we both determine to do whatever we can in the natural, with practical application, to begin restoring the relationship...if we do not realize and understand that the initial battle is a spiritual one, all of the above acknowledgements, resolutions, and actions will soon dissolve.

How many times have we tried to win spiritual battles with carnal weapons? I have seen well-meaning parents do almost anything in their efforts to maintain peace and quiet in their homes.

I remember especially one particular set of parents with whom my wife and I counseled regarding their sixteen-year-old daughter. This couple constantly flooded the girl with expensive "things" in hopes that these gifts would create some kind of bond between them and reunite their relationship.

The situation only got worse because these expensive gifts created a bigger demand in the girl's life for more extravagant "things." The more she received, the more her self-indulgence grew out of control through her heightened lust for materialism.

That couple did not totally heed our counsel and warning. They ended up giving the girl a brand new Trans Am sports car for her seventeenth birthday. The car brought hugs, kisses, and tears from both daughter and parents as they warmly embraced, mom and dad wishfully thinking that now everything between them and their child was finally settled once and for all. And from all outward appearances, things did seem to be "A-OK." However, only a few weeks later another situation arose which the young lady did not know how to cope with, so she got in her bright new sports car and used it to run away from home!

This incident illustrates a point. There is nothing wrong with giving children nice things. But gift giving is wrong when it becomes an attempt to utilize "things" as a means of healing broken relationships. The gift and the warm feelings it produces may bring a moment of peace, but it is only temporary. Sooner or later, the same forces which produced the problem in the first place will once again flare up, provoking bitter disappointment in the parents and resentment in the child.

Natural weapons will never win spiritual battles.

The Spirit of Fear

Alcoholics Anonymous has made a great contribution in helping those who are slaves to alcohol. Thousands have been able to quit drinking through this commendable program. However, the alcoholic in the program has a lingering fear that he may one day return to that same empty, destructive way of life because he is told that he is still alcoholic.

The spiritual problem of the alcoholic has not yet been fully faced and dealt with. If it had, that fear would be gone and there would be complete mental and spiritual freedom as well as physical freedom.

You see, I was completely delivered from the bondages of alcohol and drugs to the extreme that I didn't even have a desire to continue in them! I was delivered through the mighty Name of Jesus, a spiritual weapon far superior to the strongholds of the devil.

Think about how many thousands attempt to overcome their feelings of inferiority by a new hairstyle, a new outfit or wardrobe, a bigger home, a higher paycheck, a career promotion, etc. Yet the root problem still remains, because it is *interior.* These people will never truly overcome that mountain of inner fear until they start to find themselves in Christ and begin to see themselves as God sees them.

Again, *natural weapons will never win spiritual battles.*

The Spirit of Rebellion

Rebellion is not a simple facial expression or a mere "snotty" attitude. Rebellion is a spiritual force which, through the generations, has cleverly weaved its way into the youth of our nation.

Pride and rebellion are the two major sins which caused Lucifer's fall. He was lifted up because of his beauty. Because he desired to be like the Most High God, he plotted to overthrow the throne. Lucifer was the instigator of the greatest rebellion time has ever recorded.

Today, Lucifer (known to us as Satan) is still the master deceiver. Even though Jesus has stripped him of his power, he still deceives millions of people — especially young people — by leading them into rebellion against any form of rightful authority.

This spirit of rebellion dominates schools in many parts of the world today. School administrators around the globe are constantly searching for new and better methods to remedy the serious problem of student insurrection.

This spirit of rebellion thrives in rock concerts worldwide, as well as in any other gathering of vulnerable youth. *To be vulnerable* means "to be open to attack." The scriptures clearly teach us that our enemy, the devil, roams around like a roaring lion, seeking someone to seize and devour. (1 Pet. 5:8.) The majority of teens caught up in the spirit of rebellion have no idea that they have fallen prey to the enemy of our souls. They are in desperate need of being released from the snares of bondage.

If a person only cuts off the heads of the irritating dandelions which grow in his yard, he will be rid of them for a while only to find them returning in greater strength. In order to completely rid an area of dandelions, it is necessary to get to the root and remove it completely.

In the same way, if you and I are ever to rid our society of the scourge of teenage rebellion, we must get to the root of the problem — which is a spirit.

But we must be discerning here. There is a difference between voicing an opinion, disagreeing, and rebellion. We need to give our young people room to grow. One way we do this is by allowing them to voice their opinions, disagree with us on certain subjects, and make some decisions on their own.

We can know that rebellion has entered the picture when we begin to notice in our youngsters a constant, open resistance to authority or control.

To begin to see your child come out of his present state of rebellion, you, the parent, must get serious about God. You must be determined that you are going to see this thing through to victory — come hell or high water!

Consistency is vital. Notice that I did not say *perfection*; I said *consistency*.

In times of stress and disunity, someone in the family needs to be stable and rock solid. Someone needs to stand against the power and deception of the spiritual enemy. As the parent in the family, that "someone" must be *you*!

Breaking the Power of the Enemy

In whom the god of this world (Satan) hath blinded the minds of them which believe not,

lest the glorious gospel of Christ, who is the image of God, should shine unto them.

2 Corinthians 4:4

It's time to grab the dandelion by the root!

If your teenager is still an unbeliever, then it is apparent that he is being blinded from seeing the light that will set him free. That power of darkness must be broken before your child can walk in the freedom you know he deserves.

On the other hand, if your teen has accepted the Lord but is living in a rebellious state, there is also a power that is blinding him and holding him back from walking in the fullness of God. It is keeping him from fulfilling the will of God in his life.

At this point, especially in the more extreme cases, most young people are unable to break themselves free from bondage on their own. They need help. They are not strong enough to pull out alone.

To break this spiritual stronghold of rebellion, you must make use of the spiritual weapons at your disposal. The Name of Jesus, the authority given you to use His Name, accompanied by the sword of the Spirit which is the Word of God — these are the weapons that will lead you to victory over all the power of the enemy!

In James 4:7, the Bible tells us that if we resist the devil, he will flee from us. In Mark 16:17 we learn that believers can cast out demons by using the Name of Jesus.

...For this purpose the Son of God was manifested, that he might destroy the works of the devil.

1 John 3:8

[God] disarmed the principalities and powers ranged against us and made a bold display and public example of them, in triumphing over them in Him and in it [the cross].

Colossians 2:15 AMP

Satan has been defeated and he must submit to and obey every command given him in the Name of Jesus. Jesus has given you, as one of His followers, authority to use His Name over all the works of the enemy.

It's time to get mad at the devil!

What would you do if you woke up in the middle of the night to find a burglar helping himself to the fine things you have worked so hard to accumulate. You wouldn't just say to yourself, "Oh, it's just a burglar," and then crawl back into your bed. No! You would call the police, get out your gun, yell for help — or something!

Nobody likes the feeling of being "ripped off." Most of us *do* something about it when we can.

What about your family? What about the joy, fun, laughter, peace, and unity that this thief has stolen right out from under your nose? Are you just going to sit back and wait until this menace "passes over" or "goes away"?

If that has been your attitude and approach to the problem of teenage rebellion in your home, then you have been deceived. One of Satan's greatest deceptions is to convince people that he does not exist.

I am not saying that we are to blame the devil for everything that goes wrong in our lives. Sometimes we are at fault ourselves. Sometimes our troubles are caused by other people or events beyond our control. But when it comes to the spirit of rebellion, if you and I do not deal with the spiritual forces behind the scene, we will continue to suffer needlessly and helplessly.

When I was in rebellion as a teenager, my mom and dad got mad at the devil. They did something about the situation. They took "affirmative action." You and I have that same right.

In Matthew 11:12 we read where Jesus told His disciples: **And from the days of John the Baptist until now the kingdom of heaven suffereth violence, and the violent take it by force.** How badly do you want your family to operate in the fullness of God, free from the spirit of rebellion and division? Badly enough to get mad? Badly enough to get violent? Do you want the kingdom of heaven badly enough to take it by force?

No, you are not to get mad at your family, of course, but at the devil and his demons. You are to take authority over them.

The true rendering of this scripture implies that those believers who are serious about success in Christ, in all areas of their lives, will take the kingdom of heaven "by force" ...as a precious prize. In other words, the answers we need, the provision and wisdom we are looking for, and much more, can all be found in the kingdom of God which is within us — in Christ.

Another translation phrases the last part of this verse, "...and the violent get restless." *To be restless* means "to be always active and inclined to action." It means "to be discontented." It means "to be disturbed until change comes"!

Never get comfortable when you know the enemy is "stomping" on your household! It's time to get mad at the devil and get the Word of God working for you in regard to your family. *Take the kingdom of God by force!*

This statement implies prompt action in the spiritual realm. It doesn't mean that you increase your forcefulness toward your teenager, but toward the forces of darkness!

After Mom and Dad started getting mad at the devil, they repented for anything they felt they had done to cause my rebellious state. First, they got their own guilt off their heart.

Second, they got into the Word of God to find His promises regarding the family.

Before you begin to resist the devil and break his hold over your children, you must have solid ground on which to stand. If you don't, then when Satan comes against you (and he will) with his reasoning power, feelings of guilt, and temptations to compromise, you will fall by the wayside and settle for less than what God has planned for you! But if you prepare yourself and get God's Word into your heart, then when Satan comes with his old bag of tricks, you will stand firm and be able to resist him on every hand! (Eph. 6:10-18; Matt. 7:24-29.)

The following are promises from God's Word regarding the family. Get them into your heart: Deut. 30:19; Luke 1:17; Ps. 91:10; Prov. 24:3,4,15; Ex. 12:23; Prov. 12:7; 21:20; Acts 2:38,39; 16:30-32.

Once my mother and father had received the Word of God into their hearts, they were ready to break the power of the enemy over the lives of their children, of which I was the most rebellious.

Several years after my salvation experience, through which I was delivered from the spirit of rebellion, I talked to my parents to find out how they had prayed for me. They shared with me the basics of what and how they had prayed. I am so excited to be able to share that information with you.

Prayer works. If your spouse is a believer, let me encourage you to get him or her to read this chapter — the entire book, if possible — then to pray this prayer with you. There is great power and unity when a husband and wife agree together in prayer.

Each place where there is a blank space in the following prayer, write in the name of your child (or children) for whom you are praying. Now, in the Name of Jesus, allow this prayer to become your very own as you stand in the gap for those precious ones God has given to you:

"Father, I/we come to You in the Name of Jesus, standing on the promises You've given me/us concerning my/our family. Your will for my/our family is for us to walk in unity and love, free from all forces of darkness.

"Now in the Name of Jesus, backed by the authority of Your Word, Father, I/we take authority over the devil and the spirit of rebellion which he has brought in the life of _____. I/we break the strongholds of darkness over _____'s life NOW!

"Satan, I/we command you in the Name of Jesus to remove your deceptive influence and cease from blinding _____'s mind

any longer. I/we proclaim now that
_____ is free
to receive the glorious light of the Gospel
of Christ and that he/she is free from the
spirit of rebellion.

"I thank You, heavenly Father, that
Your Word is working mightily in the life
of _____. Amen."

God is now on the scene. The Name
of Jesus has been applied, and Satan
must flee. You have used your spiritual
weapons on the spiritual enemy, and
faith has gone into effect.

Now the key is to keep our eyes on
the Word no matter how things may look
in the natural. You can read in the
Gospels that when Jesus ministered to
those who were demon-possessed, the
devil threw them on the ground and
caused them to look even worse than they
did before Jesus arrived on the scene. The
devil doesn't want to leave any situation
over which he has been in control.

I am not, by any means, implying here
that your son or daughter is demon-

possessed. But it is obvious that darkness has prevailed in some way and to some exent in your child's life. Since you have applied the Word of God to that situation, things may seem to get worse before they get better...but don't allow appearances to cause you to doubt or waver.

In my case, things did get somewhat worse before they were turned around. The devil was upset because he knew that his days of control over my life were numbered.

The key now is to stand and allow the Holy Spirit to begin His special work: **...and having done all, to stand** (Eph. 6:13).

Dare to trust God!

5

God Can Use Others Too!

"Therefore beseech the Lord of the harvest to send out workers into his harvest."

Matthew 9:38 NAS

Has the thought ever crossed your mind that if you don't do it all or say it all then it won't get done or said?

Regarding the return of our wayward children to the Lord, this thought is a common one. But it's not absolutely accurate. Sure there are many things that our children depend completely upon us their parents for, but when it comes to seeing our children's lives transformed by Christ, we must have total, unwavering faith in Him and His other workers.

Something else that my parents did which greatly contributed to my repentance was to pray that the Lord would send forth laborers, or workers, into the harvest field of my life.

I can remember times at the park, at the airport, and in my own neighborhood when someone would come up to me "from out of the blue" and share something with me about Jesus. At times I would find myself glancing over a religious tract or watching some preacher on television for a minute or two. One time I even found myself at a Christian concert in which Andre Crouch and the Disciples were playing.

Never underestimate the power of God. He has more than one way to get the job done. Most prodigal sons and daughters who eventually come to their senses and return home do so because someone, or something, somewhere "hit the magic button," as we might say, stirring in them a repentant heart, which in turn caused them to begin their long journey home.

Ask the Lord to send forth laborers into the harvest field of your child's life. Pray that everywhere he goes — whether at work, at school, during free time, with friends — he will run into someone who loves the Lord, someone who will share that love with him. Pray that God will continue to send workers across your child's path until he comes home and gets right with the Lord.

You see, God can use others too.

Think about how God so loved the Ethiopian eunuch that he sent Philip running after his chariot to preach the Gospel to him. Right then and there the eunuch got saved. I'm sure that fellow had a mother somewhere who was praying for him.

It's interesting to note in this story, which is found in Acts 8:26-40, that God sent Philip to this man at the very moment he was "ripe for picking." When Philip noticed that he was reading from the Prophet Isaiah, he asked him if he understood what he was reading. The Ethiopian's response is one which I am sure the entire human race must cry out from time to time in their search for God:

And he said, "Well, how could I (understand) unless someone guides me?" And he invited Philip to come up and sit with him.
Acts 8:31 NAS

There comes a certain time in the life of each one of us when we hunger for God. Even the sinner hungers from time to time for the truth about God, especially as his sins grow old and cold. It is at this point that God places His messenger on the scene, whether it be angel or human. Wherever there is a hungry heart, God will make sure someone is there to plant the seed, water it, or reap the harvest.

Knowing this truth brings a bit more peace to the heart of a parent who is in the midst of a battle with or for a troubled teen.

That's right, by no means are you "on your own."

God can — and will — use others to help.

Aren't you glad?

6
Cast Your Care on the Lord

Now that you've broken the power of the enemy and prayed for the Lord to send laborers into the life of your child, it is time to give this thing into the hands of the Lord — for good.

Cast the care of your child on the Lord.

Before we can go any further, it is vitally important for you to release the care, anxiety, and pressures this situation might have brought into your life. Place it all upon the Lord's shoulders, **casting all your care upon him; for he careth for you** (1 Pet. 5:7).

The following paragraphs were written by my father, Jim Glassford, with the help of my mother, Marge. To better relate to the hearts of the parents faced with teenage rebellion, I asked my own parents to share in this section. Since they have been there themselves, having dealt with four children who today are all living gloriously for Jesus, serving Him in the ministry, I felt that their viewpoint on this subject might be interesting as well as beneficial. This is what they had to say:

"Our greatest test was in the area of standing. The Bible says that we are to cast all of our cares upon God. Why should we do that? Because He cares for Jim and Marge.

"One of the ways we would do this is by praying in the Spirit. Whenever a thought of worry, concern, or fear would enter our minds regarding one of our children, we would simply begin praying in the Spirit. By praying in that heavenly prayer language, we didn't violate the prayer of faith that we prayed over the lives of our children.

"The Bible says that when we pray in the Spirit our mind is unfruitful, or, our mind is unaware of what our spirit is praying. But I believe in the prayer of the Spirit, that the Spirit of God can accurately pray, upon the earth, concerning the immediate circumstances of your child.

"During this period of time that we were believing for our children to come into the Kingdom, we had many opportunities to stumble, fall, not stand strong, and worry. The activities of our oldest son, Greg, were ever burdensome upon our lives as he was by far the most rebellious child, living for himself and following after the way of the world step by step.

"I want to share with you an event which happened during this period of time we were standing. Our two youngest children, Brian and Brenda, had already come to know the Lord. Our oldest son, Greg, and our eldest daughter, Debbie, were both still living in Orlando, Florida, after we had moved to Tulsa, Oklahoma.

"Greg was working and partying, while Debbie was attending a junior college and partying, studying to be a nurse. Debbie was always cheerful and the apple of her daddy's eye. She was faithful to phone Tulsa and report of her activities. Debbie was always a joy to be around and talk to. However, once you

come to know the Lord, your spirit is
changed and your life is full of the Holy
Ghost. You're walking to the beat of a
different drummer.

"In conversations over the months
with my daughter, I began to recognize
the confusion that was in her life. She
would continually change her mind
regarding various activities and relationships. After hanging up from one such
phone conversation, I was particularly
grieved concerning her. All throughout
the rest of that day I was meditating of
how I could help her come to know the
Lord. If I could just get her to Tulsa…

"That night I was moved to pray even
more for my daughter. As I lay before the
Lord, I began to feel the heaviness and
care. Somehow I had taken the care of my
children off of the Lord's shoulders and
placed it on mine again. I was trying to
'figure out' how I was going to rescue my
kids. In the midst of my prayer time, I saw
something that turned the entire situation
around.

"Within my spirit I had a vision. I saw
the Lord Jesus sitting on a very beautiful

chair looking directly into my eyes. And suddenly, upon His lap, appeared my daughter, Debbie. Then the Lord said these life-changing words to me, '*I am more than enough.*'

"Something beautiful began to overwhelm my soul and *I knew* that everything was going to be all right for both my daughter and my son, Greg.

"The Lord knew that I was wavering. I hadn't fallen, I was still standing, but I was wavering. He knew that I was about to interrupt the plans that He had made for the lives of my children. From that point on I was to leave the care upon Him and trust Him to continue to work in their lives and bring them into His Kingdom.

"Needless to say, from that day forward, after I related this incident to my wife, Marge, we stood firmly, unfaltering, without shaking, and without falling. Within a few short months' time, both Debbie and Greg came to beautifully know the Lord Jesus Christ. Today, both of them, and their spouses, have not only attended Bible school, but they are also serving the Lord in full-time ministry. Most importantly, they are obeying the will of God for their lives.

"Praying isn't the test...

"Believing isn't the test...

"STANDING IS THE TEST."

Right now is the time to cast the whole of your care upon the Lord. *He is more than enough to watch over your child and bring you the peace and comfort you need.* But He can only do these things if you are willing to unload the care — let go and let God.

Begin to see your son or daughter sitting on the lap of Jesus. See the Lord look into your eyes and say, "I am more than enough."

"In Jesus' Name, I pray that you be free from weariness, worry, fear, stress, and heaviness. In Jesus' Name, I pray that you be filled with the fruit of the Spirit, confidence, joy, freshness, and that you get the spring back into your step, the smile back on your lips and in your heart, and the glory back in your walk which the devil has tried to steal from you.

"In Jesus' Name...BE FREE!

"I also pray that God will restore respect for you if you feel you have lost it concerning your children. Respect is not demanded, respect is earned. I pray that the wisdom and understanding of the Holy Spirit will saturate your heart and mind as you prepare to make new decisions regarding your family relationships. Amen."

There will be times when you will be tempted to take everything into your own hands and bypass the knowledge and leading of the Lord. The pressure will seem so great at times that it will attempt to push you into making hasty and unwarranted decisions. Let me exhort you to "haste not." Instead, let **...the peace of God, which surpasses all comprehension, ...guard your hearts and your minds in Christ Jesus** (Phil. 4:7 NAS).

Through what we have shared in this chapter, we are not at all implying that you should just sit back and do absolutely nothing while the devil runs amok through your household. No, no, no. That is getting over in the other ditch.

God will lead you concerning all things. You must obey Him and do what He says. As you trust and obey, fixing your eyes on Him, you will be able to see the end result, knowing that the present circumstances are only temporary.

7

Framing Your Teen with the Word

In the regions of arctic America and Greenland lives an animal called the musk ox. There is something quite peculiar about the behavior of this fellow which is rarely seen in the rest of the massive animal kingdom.

When an individual musk ox has been hurt, or grown weak or sickly, the rest of the herd bands together to protect him. When they sense danger approaching, a number of brother musk oxen, by instinct, will back close to the disabled friend. Facing outward toward the attacker, they will form a complete circular wall of defense and protection around the weaker member of the herd.

If the enemy actually attacks, the strong musk oxen, equipped with large heads, sturdy bodies, and sharp horns similar to those of the water buffalo, will fight to the death. Often these powerful animals will destroy the attacker while their fellow ox remains defended, unharmed, and on the road to recovery.

There is a way that parents of a hurting teenager can become the strength that teen needs. They can surround their youngster with a shield of faith and love so powerful that no adversary can ever hope to penetrate it.

Faith: Trusting in the Invisible Power of God

Jesus saith unto him, Thomas, because thou hast seen me, thou hast believed: *blessed are they that have not seen, and yet have believed.*

John 20:29

Now faith is the evidence of things hoped for, the evidence of things not seen.

Through faith we understand that the worlds were *framed by the word of God,* so that things which are seen were not made of things which do appear.

Hebrews 11:1,3

It is easy to become discouraged and lose hope when we constantly look only at the things we see in our rebellious teenagers. All of the negative traits always seem to rise to the surface to flood our minds, focus our concentration, and affect our viewpoint. The positive traits, on the other hand, often seem to be few and far between.

In order to keep a positive outlook and attitude while standing in faith for your teenager to come around, it is important to begin seeing him as God sees him. To do that, it is necessary to develop a new image within your heart.

In the past, you've probably been looking only through your natural eyes. Perhaps it has been difficult to see anything other than the everyday attitudes of rebellion, disrespect, anger, bitterness, strife, and rejection. You may have been overwhelmed by some of your child's bad habits, which might include cursing, drinking, smoking, lying, stealing, drug use, or a number of other negatives. You might have wondered if his behavior is ever going to change. The problem probably seems to get bigger every day! What are you going to do?

Magnify the Promise, Not the Problem

Remember, you have taken authority over the devil. You have asked the Lord to send forth laborers into your child's harvest field. And you have cast all of your cares upon the Lord. Now it is time to start *acting as though what you believe is true*. It is time to act like God, Who **...calleth those things which be not as though they were** (Rom. 4:17).

It's time to *frame your teenager with the Word of God.*

God stands behind each and every promise He has set forth in His Word. In the Old Testament, the Lord spoke to Jeremiah and said, **"...I am watching over My word to perform it"** (Jer. 1:12 NAS). In Isaiah 55:11 NAS He states: **"So shall My word be which goes forth from My mouth; it shall not return to Me**

empty, without accomplishing what I
desire....without succeeding in the
matter for which I sent it."

If God said these things, then we
must dare to believe and act as though
they are true — because they are true!
Instead of continuing to see your child
only through your natural eyes, you must
begin to see him as God sees him. A new
image will begin to be birthed within you
as, in your spirit, you start to see your
child saved, obedient, full of respect for
himself and you, full of the fruit of the
Spirit, loving life, and filled with a
burning desire to serve the Lord Jesus
Christ.

Even though, when you look at or talk
with your child, he is blatantly rebellious,
obviously confused, or openly cynical
and critical, be continuously thanking the
Lord within yourself that those physical
expressions and reactions are *subject to
change*!

When you pray for your child, remove
from your mind the image of sin and
rebellion which you've had of him in the

past. Begin to see that child with a countenance of life. See him with a godly smile, motive, and desire.

That is the way our heavenly Father sees us. The Apostle Paul wrote to the believers of his day:

Blessed be the God and Father of our Lord Jesus Christ, who has blessed us with every spiritual blessing in the heavenly places in Christ,

just as *He chose us in Him before the foundation of the world, that we should be holy and blameless before Him....*

Ephesians 1:3,4 NAS

God, our heavenly Father, believes in us. He sees us living in total obedience to His Word. This doesn't mean that He ignores the sin in our lives; He knows our every thought. But at the same time, He never gives up believing that we can make it. He always sees us in the image of His Son.

Begin to *speak the Word over your child.* Frame him, as it were, with the Word of life. Surround him with faith that erupts from the Scriptures.

Every day my wife Lisa and I plead
the blood of Jesus over our two boys
Matthew and Nicholas. We speak forth
that they are obedient to their parents and
to the Lord. We say that they are the head
and not the tail, that they are above and
not beneath. We say that they shall find
favor in the sight of God and man all the
days of their lives. We call forth the Spirit
of God to live big in them. We say that
the fruits of the Spirit will be evidenced
in them every day of their lives, and that
they will live to give.

We say of our sons that they will be
taught of the Lord, and that great will be
their peace. We continue to speak forth
that Matt and Nick will fulfill everything
that God has called them to do before the
return of Jesus Christ.

We even are starting to call forth godly
wives for our sons, speaking forth
blessings over their future mates whom
God has already chosen for them.

We are beginning to shape the seen
with the unseen.

Regarding your rebellious teenager, you can begin to do the same thing by determining to never, ever call him rebellious again. Instead, call him obedient. Begin to speak forth that your child will start to rebel against the devil instead of against his parents and God!

Begin to frame your teen with the Word of God and watch the natural begin to come into line with the supernatural.

I am not talking about speaking these things to his face. I am talking about your saying them as you walk in your house, go to your job, when you are lying down, or out on the golf course. Wherever you are, speak the Word of God over your teen!

The world's system has taken its toll on your child in some way. It's time to apply God's system which will mold him into the righteous one He has called him to be.

As you speak the Word of God over your teenager, he will begin to be influenced first in the realm of the spirit.

Eventually, he will begin to think differently. Sooner or later, he will find himself thinking twice about the sin he so easily gave into not so long ago.

God's Word, conceived in your heart, formed on your lips, and spoken out of your mouth, becomes a spiritual force which releases the ability of God within you! (Read that one again!)

God's Word is creative! God's Word *works*!

In Proverbs 22:6, parents are told: **Train up a child in the way he** *should* **go....** If there is a way a child *should* go, then there is also a way he *shouldn't* go.

In raising our children, we are commanded by God to speak the Word *to them*. Let's look at Deuteronomy 6:5-7 in the *New American Standard Bible* for confirmation of this truth:

"And you shall love the Lord your God with all your heart and with all your soul and with all your might.

"And these words, which I am commanding you today, shall be on your heart;

"and you shall teach them diligently to your sons and shall talk of them when you sit in your house and when you walk by the way and when you lie down and when you rise up."

Framing your teen with the Word of God is simply getting him back on track, back in conformity to the will of God.

Magnify the promise — not the problem!

The more you speak the Word of God, the more it will become real to you. When faith becomes fact within you, it is a sure sign that manifested victory is just around the corner.

Rejoice!

Because you have dared to trust God, and have acted upon His Word, things are beginning to happen in the unseen world. God, Jesus, the Holy Spirit, the angels, laborers, and the mighty Word have all gone into effect on your behalf.

When Abraham was told by the Lord that Sarah would conceive and bear him a son in his old age, he glorified God because he knew that He would do what He said.

He staggered not at the promise of God through unbelief; but was strong in faith, giving glory to God;

And being fully persuaded that, what he had promised, he was able also to perform.

Romans 4:20,21

Be like Abraham. Be fully persuaded that what God has promised in regard to your child, *He* will also bring to pass!

What would you do if you found out this very moment that your teenager had turned around completely? You would probably get happy and begin to rejoice. Begin now to act as if this desired change has already taken place.

Remember, **...faith is the substance of things hoped for, the evidence of things *not* seen** (Heb. 11:1).

Has not God said it, and will He not make it good? (Num. 23:19.)

Rejoice evermore.

...for this is the will of God in Christ Jesus concerning you.

1 Thessalonians 5:16,18

8
Rules, Discipline, and Punishment: Is there a Balance?

Trying to discipline a rebellious teenager is, at times, like trying to teach a baby to ride a tenspeed bicycle over rough terrain. It just won't work.

Punishment isn't the answer either. Why? Because when you punish a wrong action, you are dealing with a symptom and not the root cause of the rebellion.

Step by Step

First of all, it is important to determine why your teen is rebelling. If there seems to be a variety of issues involved, deal with them one by one. You must pinpoint as much as possible exactly what it is your child is in rebellion against.

Almost without exception, young people do not rebel against their parents as much as they rebel against a value system, a lifestyle, or rules of behavior which the parents stand for.

For example: A close acquaintance of ours recently read a runaway note from his daughter. The note commented on how the rules of the home were too strict and unreasonable. This was the main reason for the girl's rebellion.

Sometimes a teenager may get confused because his parents keep on changing the rules and the youth does not know if he should follow the old system or the new.

Take it step by step, issue by issue. Believe for God's wisdom and guidance as you work on your standards and rules.

Let me throw in a practical suggestion here: Steer away from the word *rules* and substitute the word *guidelines*. It sounds a bit less commanding and somewhat more obtainable.

When communication breaks down, don't withdraw. Negotiation does not always spell compromise. And, while we are on the subject, compromise does not always mean backing down from the Word of God. Many times, it simply means taking a less authoritarian, less offensive approach.

When dealing with your youngster, never dominate the conversation or attempt to use force to get your way. The reason kids rebel is because they are trying to equal the balance of power. If you continually crush your child's attempts to communciate with you as an equal, you are setting yourself up for a great power struggle.

Your teen's rebellion may or may not be his own fault. But whether it is his fault or not, the responsibility for reconciliation is yours because, most likely, he will not take the first step to change things. The fact that parents are willing to change *their* attitudes and behavior communicates more to their child than anything they might do to force their way.

Can you remember times when your own parents "let up" on you a little? I certainly can, and I also remember how bad it made me feel because of my rotten attitude during our previous argument. One time I felt so bad about my behavior, I actually asked my parents to reconsider and not allow me to have the thing I was pitching a tantrum to get!

My parents did not compromise because they were tired of the "hassle." They "let up" from time to time because they saw the pressure building up in my life.

Sometimes young people need a break. Many teenagers do not realistically know how to handle the numerous pressures applied to them through school, society, friends, parents, and — at times — even the church. A parent who understands this fact is to be commended; he will certainly be rewarded — with greater success in raising his teenager.

Discipline and.Punishment: There Is a Difference

Before a parent can accurately and fairly set up guidelines and consequences, he must have a clear under-standing of what the words *discipline* and *punishment* mean.

Discipline, according to the dictionary is: a) a branch of knowledge or learning, b) training that develops self-control, character, or orderliness and efficiency, c) strict control to enforce obedience.

Some time ago I ran across another definition which is a bit more satisfactory in regard to teenagers: Discipline is the setting of a child to a task in order to exercise, strengthen, and help him to mature. For example, discipline is what an athletic coach puts a team through *before* a game.

Punishment, on the other hand, is more a matter of justice. The dictionary defines it as: "A penalty inflicted on an offender as a retribution, and incidentally for reformation and prevention." In the context of the home, punishment is something which is imposed upon a child *after* he has violated a family guideline.

So then we could say that discipline is obedience to an established system of rules of behavior, while punishment is the consequence of breaking one of those rules. For teens, a common form of punishment for "breaking discipline" is that of being grounded, or the loss of television or phone privileges.

In dealing with rebellious teens, I believe there is a need for both discipline and punishment.

Suggestions for Establishing Appropriate Discipline and Punishment

The following is a list of helps, ideas, or suggestions to consider as you re-evaluate your discipline and punishment procedures:

1. Write down your current guidelines (rules) and decide which are reasonable and which are questionable, then re-evaluate each one through prayer.

When you have compiled your list, take the time to discuss it with your teen. Remember, communication is a two-way street. Allow room for your child to comment.

2. Decide what punishment will be administered when any certain guideline is not heeded. (You may negotiate the guidelines, but be careful about negotiating the consequences.)

Often, parents tend either to make the punishment greater than the act demands, or to make it less serious than the act. Thus, the child ends up thinking that the punishment was either too severe for the act, or that it really wasn't too high a price to pay for what he did. Never be inconsiderate about punishment. Although you should not expect your teen to break the rules, it is wise to predetermine the punishment prior to the act of disobedience in order to save you from making a hasty, and possibly unfair, judgment.

For example: Your son asks if he can use the family car for an evening date. You agree, but remind him that he must be home by 10:30 p.m. or he will forfeit his right to use the car next weekend. He gets home at 11:30 p.m. with no reasonable excuse for his tardiness. A fair punishment — one equal to the act — would be to deny him use of the car next weekend, just as you had warned.

When Is Spanking Inappropriate?

The use of spanking as punishment generally levels off when the child reaches the age of about twelve to thirteen. In some cases, it might be best to stop the practice even a year or two earlier. It is difficult to draw a hard and fast line here.

As a parent, you can know when it's time for consequential discipline. If the child begins to respond with a sort of "oh, well, here we go again" attitude, then you know that the punishment will do little good. He is obviously growing up and is ready to face the next stage of discipline.

3. Make sure your teen understands *why* you have set up guidelines and principles of discipline and punishment.

The following illustration might be helpful to use to explain your reasoning to your teenager: "A skydiver may want to experience the freedom of gliding through the air without the hassle and extra weight of a parachute. He is absolutely free to do so. But he is *not free* to escape the consequences that await him at the end of his flight."

These scriptures are also beneficial:

A wise man will hear, and will increase learning; and a man of understanding shall attain unto wise counsels:

The fear of the Lord is the beginning of knowledge: but fools despise wisdom and instruction.

Proverbs 1:5,7

Poor is he who works with a negligent hand, but the hand of the diligent (faithful, hard-working, and disciplined) makes rich.

Proverbs 10:4 NAS

Many times teenagers imagine that their parents are aliens from another planet whose main purpose is to make their life miserable. Assure your teen of your love and that you are only interested in his well-being.

4. Never use discipline or punishment as a weapon.

Discipline is a tool, not a weapon. Too often, as parents, we find ourselves on the defensive, acting out of spite, irritation, or anger. If we expect punishment to yield the peaceable fruit of righteous in our children, then that punishment must be an expression of love — not of anger. (Heb. 12:7-11.) This is VITAL.

Whom God loves, He disciplines. (Heb. 12:6.) Proverbs teaches us that if we do not discipline our children, then we do not love them. (Prov. 13:24.) If your child feels he must *earn* your love, then you're in trouble. I believe that our children need to see discipline as evidence of our love.

5. Never react without first knowing all the facts.

As parents, we need to learn not to get "uptight," or to jump to conclusions. It is unwise to react without first knowing the facts. How sad it would be if we were to pass judgment on a child only to discover later that he was truly innocent of the deed for which he was punished.

Don't be too hasty to draw conclusions. Never act on suspicion. Give your child the benefit of the doubt.

6. Avoid nagging, sarcasm, and verbal "putdowns."

When you constantly nag or "put down" your child, not only are you contributing to his development of an inferiority complex, worse yet, you are sacrificing your authority. Rather than exercising true adult leadership, you are reducing yourself to his level by engaging him in a "battle of wills."

Learn to communicate, even in the midst of a trying situation.

7. Stop punishing repeated offenses.

If your teen is constantly repeating the same disobedient, rebellious act, it's time to start looking a little deeper for the root of the problem. Habitual disobedience is a symptom of more serious complications which need prompt attention.

8. Be consistent and follow through.

Too many times parents threaten some type of punishment, but then fail to follow through because it is too inconvenient to do so. Teenagers respect parents who carry out the punishments they set. If you are constantly inconsistent, your teen will soon lose all sense of respect for you. If you really carry out the punishment which you have decreed, in the love of the Lord, it will pay off in the long run.

9. Know when to involve a third party or to bring in professional help.

In his article entitled "When to Seek Professional Help," Gary D. Bennett provides an excellent guideline as to when to call for outside help in dealing with teens. When the teenager requests or indicates in other ways that he needs help, when the parent feels he can no longer handle the situation, or when the teenager exhibits chronic unhappiness; behavior problems such as lying, stealing or running away; feelings of unworthiness, or continuing depression or loneliness — the parent should seek help. If the needs of the teenager/and or family are beyond the expertise of the minister of the local church, the parent should ask his pastor to help locate an appropriate community agency and to remain in a supportive role to the family.

Besides the church, particular community agencies can be contacted for help with particular problems: For discipline — family service agencies, juvenile court, or the school counselor. For drug problems — a counselor on alcoholism, a drug crisis or treatment center, or the police department. For runaways — social and family service agencies, runaway centers, or the police department. For sexual misconduct — family service agencies.

The parent should encourage the teenager to take advantage of the community resources by making him aware of them and relating to him the importance of making and keeping appointments. The parents should explain to the teenager that he needs to seek help, not because he is sick or crazy, but to broaden his freedom of choice by providing him with more options, and that seeking help in appropriate ways is a sign of maturity. The parent will retain the right to continue or discontinue using the services and explain in detail exactly what will happen when the teenager goes to the agency.

Foster care is a temporary alternative to home care. Separation from the family provides the teenager the opportunity to look closely at himself and his behavior and provides the parents the opportunity to make changes to help develop a more meaningful relationship when the teenager returns. For teenagers with severe problems or those who are severely disturbed, "residential treatment" facilities are available. To conclude his article, Mr. Bennett points out that a parent's decision to seek professional help is not an admission of failure, but simply a recognition of a need for help.[1]

---

[1] Jay Kesler, *Parents & Teenagers.*

It should be emphasized, however, that additional, outside help can never be a complete substitute for parental authority. The Christian parent should pursue professional help only by the leading of the Holy Spirit and only from those who have a strong Christian foundation. Otherwise, he may be "jumping out of the frying pan into the fire." **Blessed is the man that walketh not in the counsel of the ungodly...** (Ps. 1:1).

10. It is so important that both parents agree on the subject of guidelines and punishment.

If you and your spouse must disagree, do so away from the ears of your teen. Your disagreement can damage your integrity in the eyes of your child, especially if he constantly sees the two of you arguing about the extremity or slackness of certain disciplinary actions. Never undo what your spouse has done. If a decision has been made by one or the other, stick to that decision and resolve your differences about it later, by yourselves, in the love of God.

9
Building a Strong Relationship With Your Teenager

While ministering at a ski retreat in Minnesota, I was talking with a young man whose father had died just about a year earlier. When I asked him about the depth of his relationship with his dad, he began to cry as he said, "He was the best friend I ever had. He was a great guy to talk to and be around."

What a loving memory. Although it is unfortunate that this young man will have to spend the rest of his life without an earthly father, it is very positive that the son's memories of his dad are those of meaningfulness, fun, and fulfillment.

This chapter could just as easily have been entitled, "Preventing Rebellion," or, "How to Prevent the Grief of Rebellious Teens."

If parents will take the time to build a strong relationship with their child while he is still young, the chances of his developing a rebellious lifestyle are slim to none. Why? Because the word *relationship* implies knowing another person — his strengths, weaknesses, fears and dreams, desires, his feelings about us.

If, per chance, you have not spent the time you should have with your child while he was growing up, let me exhort you to believe that "the glory of the latter days" of your relationship "will be greater than the glory of your former days."

In other words, begin believing that God will restore to you and your child the time that Satan has stolen from your family relationships. I can speak from experience that this miracle is positively and realistically possible! God restored to wholeness and newness the battered relationship between my dad and me.

The amount, or quantity, of time is not nearly as important as the true, genuine quality of time spent with your child. At the same time, I would like to propose this question: Is it possible to create quality time without investing quantity time?

Your spending quality time with your child says to him, "I want to spend time with you to get to know you better because I love you for who you are." To spend time with your child simply because you feel you have to (since it's been so long since you've done so) is a wrong motive. Isn't it true that we will spend both quality and quantity time with those people we love and doing those things we enjoy? Sure it is!

I can remember buying my first guitar when I was eighteen years old. My parents had bought me a guitar when I was a young boy, but there was something special about paying cash for that instrument from the money I had personally worked so hard to earn. I remember spending hours every day practicing on that new guitar. I enjoyed it and I had a real desire to learn to play it well.

In a marriage relationship, if the couple really loves each other, they will spend time together, even at the expense of other things they might enjoy. *Quality time is the result of quantity time.* In a sense, they are one and the same. You really can't have one without the other. Quality time expresses a desire to want to be with the other person, while quantity time proves that desire.

True love can be measured by the size of the sacrifice made by the one who admits that love. **For God so loved the world, that he gave his only begotten Son...**(John 3:16). What a sacrifice! What a perfect, unselfish act! What an expression of pure, undefiled love!

We must realize that teenagers will not drop everything to come running at our beck and call to spend time with us at our convenience — when *we* are ready. Perhaps another cause for our teens' rebellious state is our failure to spend time together with them. Therefore, we cannot expect things to change overnight. Building a strong relationship requires

time, understanding, and communication.

**But to do good and to *communicate*, forget
not: for with such sacrifices God is well pleased.**

Hebrews 13:16

Communication is a sacrifice. To
properly communicate is a very unselfish
act. And to spend quality time with your
child will require sacrifice and
unselfishness.

Regardless of the symptoms of
rejection you might feel when you begin
the restoration process, remember: you've
formed a new image within yourself of
your son or daughter! Now is the time to
begin to walk out your faith. Now is the
time to begin acting as though what you
prayed and believe is really true. Decide
now that you will make the transition to
spend both quality and quantity time
with your teenager. You may want to ease
into it bit by bit, little by little, so that your
teen will not think that you've gone totally
berserk. Use wisdom and discretion.

The following list includes some practical tips on getting started in *building a strong relationship with your teenager:*

1. *Develop a desire to reach out.*

Without a desire to do anything, nothing will ever get done! Desire is the key to action. If you've lost the desire to reach out to your teen because your past efforts have been rejected time and again and you feel that you've exhausted your resources, let me once again encourage you — *don't give up!*

As hard as it may be to believe, *your teenager needs you!* And, just as important, you need your teenager! That's right — *you need each other!*

If you've lost the desire to move forward in this area, allow the Holy Spirit to *create a new desire with you now.*

"Then your light will break out like the dawn, and your recovery will speedily spring forth....

"And...you will rebuild the ancient ruins; you will raise up the age-old foundations; and you

will be called the repairer of the breach, the restorer of the streets in which to dwell."

Isaiah 58:8,12 NAS

Forgive your child for the hurt, humiliation, and any degradation he has brought you. Release him now in the Name of Jesus. Do not hold those things against him any longer. Reach out and take hold of the healing power of God right now. Allow that *new desire* to begin to rise up within you to strengthen you and give you hope, excitement, and vision to rebuild even a stronger relationship!

2. *Make use of affirmation.*

For a child to hear his father or mother say, "Well done," can have a far greater positive influence upon his life than we realize.

To affirm means "to say something positive; to uphold." Children have a great need for approval, praise, and affirmation. A teen realizes, although he may not admit it, that his parents know him best. If they feel good about him, then he will feel good about himself and will develop a sense of self-worth and self-esteem. The healthier his self-image, generally the more he will achieve. A teen's self-confidence — how he feels about his abilities, gifts, and talents — is usually the reflection of what his parents feel about him.

It is important to point out your child's uniqueness. Appreciate his special personality. Praise him for what he does that is good and right. When he makes an effort to excel and improve his abilities, gifts, and talents, when he fulfills his responsibilities, praise him for it — whether or not his achievements meet your standards. The point is to recognize the geniune strides and efforts he makes.

Can a parent affirm and/or praise his child too much? Never. Not if the praise and affirmation are legitimately sincere.

Let me suggest that you begin to focus on your child's strengths and not just his rebellious attitudes. Whenever there is a need for you to correct him, point out why what he did was wrong. But then

always come back with something
positive that he is doing. As the old
saying goes, "Good can be found in
everything."

I have ministered to some kids whose
parents had degraded them so much for
the wrong they had done that the
youngsters didn't think that God could
ever forgive them. They were afraid and
ashamed to take the situation to the Lord!
No situation should ever be allowed to
reach this place of hopelessness.

Balance the weaknesses with
strengths. It will give your child the hope
he needs and help him to believe in
himself.

Studies have shown that for every one
negative response or reaction of a parent
to his child, it takes at least four positive
responses to balance the scale. When we
begin to realize how quick most of us
parents are to nit-pick and criticize, and
how slow we are to praise, then we begin
to understand that too much praise is
hardly a real danger.

Besides all of these considerations, we must remember that it was God Who set up this reward system in the first place.

And without faith it is impossible to please Him, for he who comes to God must believe that He is, and that He is a rewarder of those who seek Him.

Hebrews 11:6 NAS

God is a *rewarder*! Rewards are scriptural! So then, get in the affirmation habit. It could change your life!

3. Take an interest in your teen's activities.

One way to affirm your child is by taking a genuine, active interest in his activities. This does not mean, of course, that you have to become involved in everything he is involved in. It does mean, however, that you should begin to stop, look, and listen in order to observe what interests your child.

Just the other day I sat down with my six-year-old son, Matthew, and asked him what was his favorite game, his favorite food, song, color, movie, etc. I just wanted to get to know him a little better.

I can remember times when my parents would take a special interest in something that I was good at, such as art, football, or basketball. It did something to me when they would get involved with me in those things from time to time. It caused my self-worth to grow and my desire to excel in those areas to increase.

You can think of various ways to help your child excel in his particular interests by: a) participation with him, b) providing materials to assist him, c) asking him to teach you about his favorite pasttime. As you take interest in your child's activities, not only will you be supporting him and strengthening your relationship together, you will also be planting seeds which will yield a harvest. This harvest may even reach the point that your teenager will actually begin to show an interest in some of the things you enjoy. Wouldn't that be interesting?

4. Don't be afraid to trust.

So you trusted your teenager to be home at a certain hour, to maintain certain standards of sexual purity, or to limit his spending to a set amount, but because he failed to keep his part of the bargain, you feel that your trust in him has been betrayed.

So now your heart is hurting. You're not sure that you can ever trust him again. What do you do?

First of all, it is important to identify the reason for your negative feeling. Is it because you fear what other people may think or say about *you* or *your* family? Are you disappointed in your teen because *you* know *you* taught him "better than that"? Are you angry because one of *your* rules has been broken? Or are you genuinely concerned about *your* child and the consequences that await *him* if he doesn't learn self-discipline?

Trusting your teenager always means running the risk of having that trust betrayed. But let's admit it, that is all a part of our growing up and accepting responsibility of raising children. It is primary that you utilize this breakdown in confidence as an opportunity to keep it from happening again. If it involved a serious breach of trust, then that trust will have to be regained a little at a time. Give your teen more freedom as he displays dependability.

Once again, the reward system should come into play here from time to time. Never reward proper behavior with material items, but with sincere, heart-felt appreciation.

No matter how severely rebellious a teen may be, deep within his heart there is a yearning to be trusted. As you provide opportunities for him to re-build trust, you are showing forth your unwavering faith in his ability to meet the test. Sooner or later this kind of faith will produce good results!

At this point, you may not be able to trust your teen in certain areas, but you can trust him in others. I recommend that you set up a series of steps to be taken by the youth in the areas in which he lacks your trust. Provide him a chance to regain your confidence in him step-by-step. Once he has well proven himself in that area, affirm him, and then build from that base.

Regardless of outward appearances to the contrary, trustworthiness is a character trait each teenager dreams of obtaining and dreads losing.

5. Double-date.

That's right — double-date!

Have you and your spouse ever gone out on a double-date with your teen and another youth? (If your child is under sixteen, you may not want to use the phrase *double-date* as yet, but simply encourage him or her to invite along a friend.) This could be the most interesting time of your life!

To really make this work, I suggest that you follow these guidelines:

a. Decide that on this "date" you will not act like a parent but like a friend (unless an unexpected situation arises which demands parental control).

b. Go "dutch" (that is, you pay for your share of the evening's expense, and your teenager pays for his share).

c. Agree ahead of time on the location and activity.

d. Talk about things that interest everybody involved (do your homework and find out what things — food, soft drinks, sports, school activities, movies, etc. — interest your teen and his date).

e. Pray at the end of the date.

The amount of time involved is unimportant. Don't prolong the date unnecessarily, but on the other hand, don't come back home after only fifteen minutes. Give your teen a chance to observe a side of you he may never have seen before. It may just "freak him out"!

6. Communicate.

"Open communication causes less complications."

— Greg Glassford

Strong relationships are dependent upon good communication. I do not believe there is a "generation gap." But I do believe there has been a devastating "communication gap." Good communication consists of openness, friendliness, and honesty.

When a problem situation arises, stop and communicate. Communication involves hearing both sides of the story and determining justice through prayer.

Communication is sitting down to breakfast, lunch, or dinner as a family and engaging in *conversation*. Begin to make it a family tradition in your home to share at least one meal together per day. With the busy schedules of both adults and teens these days, life can become so hectic that a family could easily go through their child's entire teenage years without ever taking a meal together at the same table.

If your home has become nothing more than a hotel and restaurant where your child stops off to eat and sleep while running through a continuous cycle of endless outside activities, then you have some serious re-evaluation to do.

Listening is vital to communication. Allow room for your child to explain his side of the issue at hand. Sometimes our adult perspective can be limited in scope. You might be surprised how much insight your teen can bring on a subject, if given the chance.

Practice honesty. Have your ever shared some of your own personal conflicts with your teenager? I don't mean the ones that he is causing! Maybe your struggle on the job, or your relationship with a co-worker, or a challenging situation with a neighbor. It just might serve you well to approach your teen and *ask his advice.*

That's right, ask what he would do if he were in a similar situation. This candid approach may well strengthen the bond between you and your teenager by allowing him to see that you are a real person with some real problems of your own.

Like any other project, building a strong relationship with your teenager will require some hard work and sacrifice. But ultimate success is not only worth it, it is assured. Let your motto be that of the

Apostle Paul who wrote: **Now thanks be unto God, which always causeth us to triumph in Christ...**(2 Cor. 2:14).

10
The Love That Never Fails

**But now abide faith, hope, love, these three;
but the greatest of these is love.**

1 Corinthians 13:13 NAS

In verse eight of this same chapter, the
Word of God does it again. It reveals a
powerful truth which our carnal mind
delays to comprehend. It declares: **Love
never fails...** (NAS).

What kind of love never fails? The
God-kind of love — *agape* love. This is the
kind of love that will make up the
difference and take up the slack when
people fall short. This God-kind of love
enables us to see others as valuable and
precious both to God and to us.

Agape love is an *unconditional* love. No
matter how things may look or what your
child has done, this special love of the
Father quickens you to look beyond the
present — with its mischief, mistakes, or
even evil — and see the future!

The *agape*, unconditional love will help you truly love your teenager no matter how he looks at this moment, no matter how great his current liabilities, no matter what may be his present attitudes and actions.

This does not mean that you will always like or approve of everything he says or does. The *agape* love of God simply assures that you will inwardly love your child even when you abhor his outward behavior.

In an earlier chapter, we stressed the importance of beginning to form a new mental image of your teen in the light of God's Word. Without *agape* love, this is an absolute impossibility.

We need to love our children not for *how* they are, or for *what* they are, but for *who* they are.

First of all, they are God's creation. God is their Father and He has a wonderful plan for their lives. As parents, it is our responsibility, delegated to us by the Divine Owner of the children, to prepare them to fulfill their mission in this life.

Second, they are individuals, not robots. Each child is a unique creation equipped with a "variety pack" of personality traits, mannerisms, and other individual characteristics which make him different from every other person on earth.

I think that from time to time we get tunnel vision and never get to really appreciate and enjoy the fun person our child was created to be. Sometimes teenagers' true personalities are repressed because of the undue pressures and strains which are often placed upon them by family and society. As unfortunate as it is, some teens will grow up and spend their entire lives under oppression, thus, never fully expressing the God-like qualities He intended for them to demonstrate and enjoy.

It is of paramount importance that you see your child as a unique, individual creation of God. To do that you must view him in the framework of the highest kind of love — *agape.*

Agape Love Is Genuine

We all long for the love that comes straight from the heart. To say "I love you" is great, and should be done, but that in itself is not enough. Your child sees your love for him by what you *say* and by what you *do*, but *what you do carries more weight.* Youths are far more affected by actions than by words.

The Lord Jesus said it this way:

…"If anyone loves Me, he will keep My word: and my father will love him, and We will come to him, and make Our abode with him.

"He who does not love Me does not keep My words…."

John 14:23,24 NAS

Could it be possible that those who do not love the reading and study of the Word of God cannot truly love the Lord? According to these verses, confirmed by others, that is precisely so!

Love is more than just words, *love is action.* If I say to my wife, "Honey, I love you," that is an expression of affection. But what if I never show my love for her by my actions? What if I never do things with her or for her, if I never spend any time with her, if I never give her nice gifts or take her anywhere with me? Sooner or later, she will begin to question my verbal expression of love for her.

If we really love with the God-kind of love, it is imperative that we *act out our love* and thus back up our words with gesture. You've heard it said time and again, "Actions speak louder than words."

Surface love is motivated by a sense of obligation: "I have to spend time with my child because I haven't done so in two weeks." It is good to think that way, but you must make sure that your feeling of obligation and need is backed by a sincere desire to spend that time. Otherwise your child will sense your true feelings and will know that you'd really rather be doing something else.

If you honestly don't enjoy spending time with your child, then you need to start making adjustments to your attitude so you won't feel that way. Parental love must be genuine.

True Love Confronts

You may have found yourself thinking sometimes that things would be better if your child were just left alone to take care of himself. However, the Word of God says, **...a child left to himself bringeth his mother to shame** (Prov. 29:15). In that same chapter we are also told, **Correct your son, and he will give you rest; yes, he will give delight to your heart** (v. 17).

One of the areas regarding rebellious teenagers which seems to be the most confusing to troubled parents is that of knowing how to deal with problem situations. We've given some practical guidelines in this book for you to consider in prayer. True love will never avoid confrontation, but will consider, through the wisdom of God, how to approach each situation in order to bring about a positive and satisfying resolution.

Faithful are the wounds of a friend; but the kisses of an enemy are deceitful.

Proverbs 27:6

You are a friend to your teen. Thus, you desire the best for him. Begin to speak forth that the wisdom of the Lord will lead you to respond with just the right words at just the right time.

Like apples of gold in settings of silver is a word spoken in right circumstances.

Proverbs 25:11 NAS

It has always amazed me to observe the wisdom of the Lord speaking through my lips when disciplining my children. It seems to be just the right word at just the right time. I know that I could not think that quickly myself — it must be the Holy Spirit!

Do not fear confrontation. But know that in order for the peaceable fruits of righteousness to grow in your child, you must confront and discipline by the *agape* love from above.

True Love Bears All Things, Believes All Things, Hopes All Things, Endures All Things

In conclusion, when things seem to be getting worse instead of better, resist the temptation to "throw in the towel." Lift up your head and remind yourself that you are not alone. The Lord will never leave you nor forsake you. He is with you and in you. And since this is true, His love is there also.

Reach down inside of yourself and lay hold upon that promised inner resource. Rely totally upon the greatest love you possess to see you through these tough times.

If tempers begin to flare up, pause and get control of yourself, then quietly pray for that inner, abiding love to take control of the situation.

There will be times when you will feel you need a human shoulder to lean on. From time to time, the comfort and support of a friend can be a wonderful help in lifting your spirit and building up your confidence. Remember, you're not the only one with such problems. There are others close to you who may have gone through a very similar situation. When you do get together, don't throw a "pity party," but talk from your heart and pray.

When a teen rebels, it is so easy for a parent to become discouraged. But keep your eyes on the Father. Keep that new image of your child at the forefront of your heart and mind. Keep strongly in front of you the vision that you have for your teen. In your spirit see him living a life filled with peace, satisfaction, and joy while upon this earth. Then see him enjoying the pleasures of heaven with you forever after this life is through.

Know that everything you are doing now will contribute to seeing that vision become reality. Always remember that what you see in the natural is subject to change.

I know that exciting things are awaiting you and your family in the future. I believe, in the Name of Jesus, that the restoration of the relationship between you and your teen is even now in the miracle process.

Take heart from my own case. I am where I am today because I had parents who wouldn't let go. They would not allow the devil to steal their children.

Thanks again, Mom and Dad, for your unconditional love — it paid off.

Unconditional love will pay off for you and your child too!

Conclusion

The Teenage Rebel:
Product of a Broken Heart

Have you ever been hurt in your life? If you have not found out yet, hurt is a universal problem. Look any place in the world, and you will find that everyone has been hurt at one time or another.

It was approximately 2 a.m. when the phone awakened me out of a deep sleep. I picked up the receiver to hear the frightened voice of the mother of a member of our youth group. She was so hysterical that all I could understand was something about "the police." I asked her to let me talk to one of the officers. The policeman told me that the youth had locked himself in his bedroom after nearly destroying the house.

The young man in question had a butcher knife and was threatening to kill himself. Knowing that he meant business, the officers had asked his mother if there was anyone the young man respected enough to listen to. She gave them my name and called me. I got dressed and rushed the five miles over to their apartment on my motorcycle.

With the Lord's help and wisdom, I was able to talk the youth into opening the door and allowing me to come in and talk. After a long time of listening and talking, he handed me the knife and agreed to leave the bedroom.

This fifteen-year-old youth was one of the most rebellious teens I had ever met. When he was at home, he ran the house. His parents were divorced, and he lived with his mother, two brothers, and a sister. His brothers and sister were all younger. Time and again, he would throw things and hit one of them or his mother. But when I could get him to talk one on one, he would get gentle as a lamb most of the time.

Out of the Heart

Where does rebellion start? With a broken heart! Somewhere along the road, hurt is experienced and never resolved. Thus, it begins to fester. In the case of this troubled young man, he was brought up to believe that he was an idiot. His father had constantly yelled at him, called him "Little Fat Boy," and said, "Can't you do anything right?" and, "You'll never amount to nothin'."

Because there was no one to help him cope with his emotions, he began to build a bitterness and hatred within himself for his father. Eventually, that attitude was reflected in everything he did and toward almost everyone he was around.

This story is only one of a million which could be told today. Perhaps it may even apply to some extent to your own family situation. Whether you believe it possible or not, most of today's teens experience at least some of the frustrations evidenced in this young man's tragic life. Check to make sure that your teenager is not more troubled than you may have realized.

Outward signs of a broken heart can be recognized by one or more of the following symptoms:

1) Withdrawal, communication breakdown

2) Ungrateful outlook and manner

3) Stubborn, sulky attitude

4) Keeping of bad company — need of other rebels for encouragement and support

5) Hearty defensiveness about wrong actions

6) Finger-pointing to condemn others

7) Extreme mood changes.

Whenever one or more of these symptoms begins to show up, stop, and take a hard look at the situation. Something must be done. Most likely, the problem won't go away, but will just get worse.

A Message to You as a Parent

If you are experiencing open rebellion from your child, it is time to look back and pray about what brought it all on. When a young child goes through numerous disappointments such as broken promises from Dad or continual criticism from Mom, he will soon develop a very bitter heart. Bitterness soon causes lack of respect and loss of affection for the person causing the hurt. The child usually becomes quite disturbed and openly ungrateful.

When that child reaches age 15 or 16, his wounded, broken heart will turn into a rebellious one. Now, instead of keeping everything inside, all that hurt-turned-into-rebellion begins to come pouring out of his mouth and through his actions wherever he may go.

Most parents realize they have a real problem on their hands when they begin to witness open rebellion in their teenager. In fact, the problem has been developing for years! In response, parents usually begin making stricter rules and "tightening the rope." Hoping for a change for the better, instead they see things continue to grow worse and worse. Rather than responding to stricter rules, the child usually reacts with further rebellion.

Don't Provoke to Anger

Children, obey your parents in the Lord, for this is right.

Honor your father and mother (which is the first commandment with a promise),

That it may be well with you, and that you may live long on the earth.

Ephesians 6:1-3 NAS

The first three verses of Ephesians 6 are possibly the most popular and most used verses in Sunday school classes and youth meetings worldwide. How have we so often overlooked the verse directly following the oft-quoted "popular" ones?

And, fathers, do not provoke your children to anger; but bring them up in the discipline and instruction of the Lord.

Ephesians 6:4 NAS

Parent, take time to examine your heart. I pray that God will reveal to you any areas where you may have "provoked" your child to anger without realizing it. I urge you to determine right now to resolve the situation through love, acceptance, and forgiveness.

Many times, rebellion in a teenager is the product of a broken heart. Far too often, that broken heart has come from the teen's own parent or parents.

As you have read these words, if your heart has been touched because you realize that you have failed to set the kind of example for your child you should have, it is not too late to make amends and to save your family. The first step is to acknowledge your failure to God in prayer. Confess to Him openly that you have sinned, and tell Him that you repent of your wrong actions and attitudes.

The Apostle John reminds us that, **If we confess our sins, he is faithful and just to forgive us our sins, and to cleanse us from all unrighteousness** (1 John 1:9). No matter how miserably you may have failed your offspring, God is standing at the door of your heart to hear your prayer and to cleanse you once again. He is

ready and willing to help you start over.
He *is* the God of the *second chance*.

Prayer

Allow this prayer to become yours
right now:

*Dear God, You know my heart better than I
know it myself. I have been wrong, Lord, in
my ways. I ask You, in the Name of Jesus, Your
Son, to forgive me for my lifestyle which has
been a bad example for my family to follow. Not
only have I sinned against these whom I love
and whom You have entrusted to me, I realize
that I have been sinning against You.*

*As You forgive me for my rebellion against You,
so now I choose to forgive my offspring for
rebelling against me. Teach me to love my child
and to be patient with him even as You love
me and are patient with me as Your child.*

*Teach me Your ways of obedience and right
living, so that I may be able to teach my family
by my example as well as by my words.*

*Preserve us both, O Lord, from a spirit of
resentment, animosity, and hurt. Help me not
to provoke my child to wrath, but to bring him
up in the discipline and instruction of the Lord.
Save my family from the consequences of my
wrong and of their own. Grant us a renewed*

love, respect, and admiration for each other and for You. May Your peace reign in our home.

Thank You for hearing and answering my prayer, in Jesus' Name. Amen.

If you prayed that prayer from a sincere heart, God has begun a great work in you and your family! In the past, you may have been guilty of harming your family by your thoughts, words, and actions. Now God has forgiven you of that past and has given you a new beginning.

The final step is for you to go to your child and confess your past sins against him. Ask his forgiveness for your wrong, just as you asked God for His. Make a commitment to your child to be the example to him that God intended for you to be all along. Whatever his immediate response, go on your way rejoicing in your new life together, confident that the good work which God has begun in you — and him — He will carry through to completion.

God bless you in your new life and relationship!